Dropping In On...
Chicago

Hilarie Staton

Rourke
Educational Media

rourkeeducationalmedia.com

Before Reading:

Building Academic Vocabulary and Background Knowledge

Before reading a book, it is important to tap into what your child or students already know about the topic. This will help them develop their vocabulary, increase their reading comprehension, and make connections across the curriculum.

1. *Look at the cover of the book. What will this book be about?*
2. *What do you already know about the topic?*
3. *Let's study the Table of Contents. What will you learn about in the book's chapters?*
4. *What would you like to learn about this topic? Do you think you might learn about it from this book? Why or why not?*
5. *Use a reading journal to write about your knowledge of this topic. Record what you already know about the topic and what you hope to learn about the topic.*
6. *Read the book.*
7. *In your reading journal, record what you learned about the topic and your response to the book.*
8. *After reading the book complete the activities below.*

Content Area Vocabulary

Read the list. What do these words mean?

catalogs
factories
immigrants
industry
jazz
neighborhoods
pier
skyscrapers
swamp

After Reading:

Comprehension and Extension Activity

After reading the book, work on the following questions with your child or students in order to check their level of reading comprehension and content mastery.

1. What was Chicago like when it was first founded? (Summarize)
2. What types of things attract visitors to the area? (Infer)
3. What factors led to Chicago's growth? (Asking questions)
4. What landmarks or attractions would you most like to visit in the city? (Text to self connection)
5. Where did Chicago get its name? (Asking questions)

Extension Activity

Create a travel brochure about Chicago. Include several places visitors should see. Write short, exciting paragraphs that highlight the most interesting things about the city. And don't forget to add pictures! You can draw them or print them out from the Internet.

Table of Contents

Chicago Facts

Founded: 1837
Land area: 237 square miles (613.8 square kilometers)
Elevation: 673 feet (205 meters) above sea level
Previous names: Fort Dearborn

Population: 2.7 million
Average Daytime Temperatures:
winter: 34 degrees Fahrenheit (2.4 degrees Celsius)
spring: 54 degrees Fahrenheit (12.4 degrees Celsius)
summer: 78 degrees Fahrenheit (25.7 degrees Celsius)
fall: 60 degrees Fahrenheit (15.7 degrees Celsius)

Ethnic diversity:
African-American 32.9%
American Indian or Alaska Native .5%
Asian 5.5%
Native Hawaiian or Pacific Islander > .5%
Hispanic or Latino 28.9%
White 31.7%

City Nicknames:
The Windy City
Second City
Chi-Town
Chicagoland
City of the Big Shoulders
Hog Butcher for the World

Number of Visitors Annually: 40 million

By the Water

See the green ribbon along the shore of Lake Michigan? And the tall buildings behind it? That's Chicago, Illinois. Over two million, seven hundred thousand people live in this city.

It didn't always look like this. When French explorers arrived in the 1600s, it was a stinky **swamp**. By the Chicago River, the water did not drain away from the land. Many wild leeks grew there. It smelled so bad that the explorers called the area *Chicago*, which came from the Miami Indians' word for the smelly leeks and a striped skunk.

Chicago Notes
Chicago is called the "Windy City," but it's only the 14th windiest city in the United States.

People in Chicago enjoy the beaches and parks along Lake Michigan.

Thousands of boats fill Chicago's Lake Michigan harbors. These boats are often seen sailing on the lake.

Chicago is built at the edge of Lake Michigan. Lincoln Park runs along the lake in the northern part of the city. Walkers, bikers, and skaters use the Chicago Lakefront Trail in all kinds of weather. Others take a paddle boat on the lagoon. There are miles of beaches. At The Peggy Notebaert Nature Museum, you can build a dam or walk with hundreds of live butterflies.

Lake Michigan by the Numbers

- **Length:** 307 miles (494 kilometers)

- **Width:** 118 miles (190 kilometers)

- **Depth:** an average of 279 feet (85 meters)

- **Deepest spot:** 925 feet (282 meters)

- Third largest Great Lake

- Sixth largest freshwater lake in the world

Lake Michigan

Chicago

IL

The Potawatomi Indians traveled between Lake Michigan and the Mississippi River. They stay away in winter. It was too cold and the rivers froze.

In 1803, U.S. soldiers built Fort Dearborn. Then settlers from the east moved there. Chicago was a city by 1837. The lake was important to the city.

In 1916, Navy **Pier** was built. It stretched a half mile (.81 kilometers) into the lake. For many years, ships loaded up there. Those ships delivered Chicago's breakfast sausages, farm machines, and chewing gum all over the world.

Navy Pier is not quite the same these days. Now it's a place to have fun!

The Chicago Children's Museum is at the pier. In the summer, you can take a boat ride on the lake. At night you can watch the fireworks that explode in time to music.

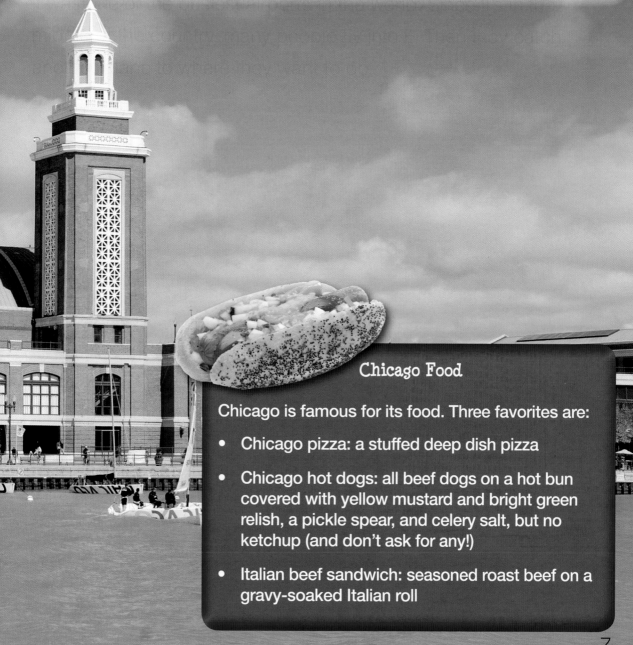

Chicago Food

Chicago is famous for its food. Three favorites are:

- Chicago pizza: a stuffed deep dish pizza

- Chicago hot dogs: all beef dogs on a hot bun covered with yellow mustard and bright green relish, a pickle spear, and celery salt, but no ketchup (and don't ask for any!)

- Italian beef sandwich: seasoned roast beef on a gravy-soaked Italian roll

The Chicago River runs through the city. It ends at Lake Michigan. You can travel across the river on one of its 45 bridges, walk along it, or explore it on a boat. There are older buildings and shiny new **skyscrapers** built beside it.

Many Chicago River bridges are movable so tall ships can use the river. When they are up, traffic on the street stops.

Meat companies and lumber mills were built near the river. They dumped their waste into the river. The waste traveled down the river into Lake Michigan. People in Chicago drank Lake Michigan water. The bad water made them sick.

It took a long time to solve this problem. Then people figured out how to make the river run backward! It doesn't dump into Lake Michigan anymore. It runs south, and canals connect it to the Mississippi River.

The Chicago River is dyed green each year for the annual St. Patrick's Day parade.

Just beyond the river is a 23-mile (37-kilometer) grassy strip called Grant Park. It runs along the lakefront. People in Chicago think of it as their front yard.

Part of it is called Millennium Park. At the park's Crown Fountain, there are 50-foot (15-meter) photos of people who live in Chicago. At Cloud Gate, also called "The Bean," you can see yourself, everyone else, and Chicago's buildings reflected on its shiny surface.

Much of Grant Park is built on rubble dumped into Lake Michigan after the Great Chicago Fire in 1871.

Chicago Notes

Grant Park is often one of Chicago's important meeting places. On November 4, 2008, Barack Obama was elected President of the United States. That night, he spoke to about 240,000 people in Grant Park. Millions around the world saw it on television and the Internet.

Sue, on display at the Field Museum, was named after the woman who discovered the skeleton, Sue Hendrickson.

The Field Museum, one of the largest natural history museums in the world, is in Grant Park. It has a famous resident: Sue, the Tyrannosaurus Rex. The skeleton is the most complete Tyrannosaurus Rex ever found.

The Art Institute of Chicago, the Adler Planetarium, and the Shedd Aquarium are also located in Grant Park.

The Art Institute of Chicago has a huge collection and an art school, where Walt Disney once took classes.

The Adler Planetarium was the first modern planetarium in the United States.

Changing City

By 1850, the United States had grown. Chicago was no longer on the western edge of the country. It was in the middle, like it is today.

At first, goods came to Chicago in boats. These trips took a long time. Then, railroads came to Chicago. By 1855, 17 different railroads arrived in Chicago. Some carried goods to the Mississippi River and the farms along the way. Others went east to Ohio and New York. The trip to Detroit, Michigan, that once took five days by water, soon took only two days.

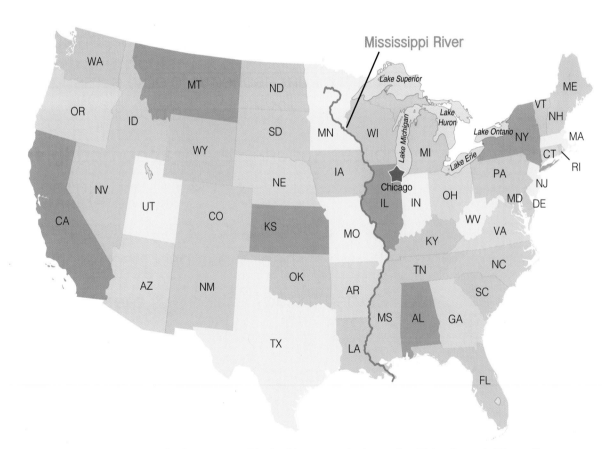

For many years, goods from New York City traveled on the Erie Canal. Then they were shipped across two Great Lakes to Chicago.

The Great Chicago Fire

The summer of 1871 was very dry. Many of Chicago's buildings were built of wood. On October 8, a fire broke out. It spread quickly. For two days, the fire raged.

After the fire, the *Chicago Tribune* published a story with the headline, "Chicago Will Rise Again." And it did. The city rebuilt quickly, but the new buildings were brick and stone, not wood.

Only a few buildings, like the tall Chicago Water Tower, survived the Great Chicago Fire.

The Great Chicago Fire of 1871

- killed 300 people
- scorched three and a half miles (5.63 kilometers) of city
- burned 17,420 buildings
- 100,000 people lost their homes

People were introduced to all kinds of new things at the Exposition, including the world's first Ferris wheel. It held 2,160 people at one time.

The World's Columbian Exposition of 1893 was held in Chicago. It celebrated the 400th anniversary of Christopher Columbus's voyage to America. It also celebrated Chicago's comeback after the fire.

Its 200 buildings were filled with interesting and exciting things. Canada sent a "monster cheese" that weighed 2,200 pounds (998 kilograms)! Visitors saw new inventions, such as the 70 foot (21 meter) tower of lightbulbs in the Electricity Building. Companies introduced new products, including Juicy Fruit gum and Cream of Wheat.

In the late 1800s, people shopped in Chicago's downtown department stores, like Marshall Fields. But many people on farms and in small towns never got to the big city to shop.

Then, companies like Montgomery Ward and Sears, Roebuck and Company, started mailing out **catalogs**. These Chicago companies sold everything from clothes to windmills. They sold watches and even kits to build entire houses. The railroads brought these goods from Chicago to farmers and small towns.

Large warehouses, like this one, held many of the goods in Montgomery Ward's catalog. Today it is being turned into stores, offices, and apartments.

Chicago started as an industrial city of **factories** and businesses. These places needed workers. Many of these workers were **immigrants** who came to Chicago looking for jobs and a better life.

At first, most immigrants to Chicago were from Ireland and Germany. Later, people came from Greece, China, and Italy. More than 17 percent of Chicago's current residents are immigrants from Mexico and other Latin American countries. Others came from India and Poland.

Many Chinese immigrants who settled in Chicago helped build the railroads.

Immigrants open stores and restaurants to sell the foods they miss from home, like the food in this Polish market.

CHICAGO HAS OVER 200 NEIGHBORHOODS AND EACH ONE IS DIFFERENT.

This mural in the Pilsen neighborhood shows today's Hispanic immigrants.

More than 75,000 African-Americans moved to Chicago between 1910 and 1940. This movement is called "The Great Migration." These people wanted better lives and jobs.

Some African-American musicians moved from New Orleans to Chicago. They brought **jazz** music with them. Chicago became famous for its jazz.

At the time, rich and poor African-Americans lived together in their own Chicago **neighborhoods**. Today, many still live in Chicago's South Side.

Many Chicago museums, like the DuSable Museum of African-American History, tell the story of the people who moved to Chicago.

People used to travel across downtown Chicago on a streetcar pulled by horses. Or they rode a cable car pulled by a strong cable or metal rope instead of a horse. Today, people crisscross Chicago on the "L," an elevated train.

Windows rattle and talking stops because it's so noisy when the "L" train goes by.

Chicago Notes

In 1882, a cable car made a loop around Chicago's downtown area. The area became known as "The Loop." Now the "L" makes a loop around nine square blocks.

21

On the 103rd floor of the old Sears Tower, now named Willis Tower, you can walk on a glass floor and see the street 1,353 feet (412.4 meters) below.

The world's first skyscrapers were built in Chicago after the Great Chicago Fire. These buildings were the first to use a steel frame. They were so tall that they needed an elevator.

Some people say that Chicago is like a museum for skyscrapers. Walk around looking up and you'll see many beautiful older ones. The new ones have more glass and steel and reach much higher.

Chicago's Midway Airport opened in 1927. Soon it was so busy, it needed an air traffic controller. This person walked around with a flag to guide the planes. But Midway had people and businesses all around it. It had no room to grow.

In 1955, Chicago-O'Hare International Airport opened. In 2014, it was one of the busiest airports in the world. Since it's in the middle of the country, many people fly into it. Then they catch another plane to where they want to go.

Famous Chicago Skyscrapers

- Home Insurance Building; 1885; 10 stories; first skyscraper, torn down in 1931

- Wrigley Building; 1924; 30 stories; clock is on 24th and 25th floors; two buildings connected by a skywalk

- Tribune Tower; 1925; 36 stories; the outside has bits of stone from important places all over the world, like the Pyramids of Egypt and the Great Wall of China

- John Hancock Center; 1969; 100 stories; each X brace is 18 stories long

- Sears Tower (now Willis Tower); 1974; 110 stories; world's tallest building when built

Wrigley Building

Chicago Sports

At a Chicago Cubs baseball game, it's easy to hear the love fans have for their team! The Cubs have won more than 10,000 games, but have not won a World Series since 1908. The Cubs play at Wrigley Field, the second-oldest major league baseball park in the United States.

The White Sox play baseball across town at the U.S. Cellular Field. In 2005, the team won the World Series. This was 88 years after the last time they won.

WRIGLEY FIELD IS SO SMALL THAT DURING ONE GAME, TWO BASEBALLS WERE HIT OUT OF THE PARK. THEY BOTH HIT THE SAME CAR PARKED ON A NEARBY STREET!

Wrigley Field was built in 1914. It didn't get lights for night games until 1988.

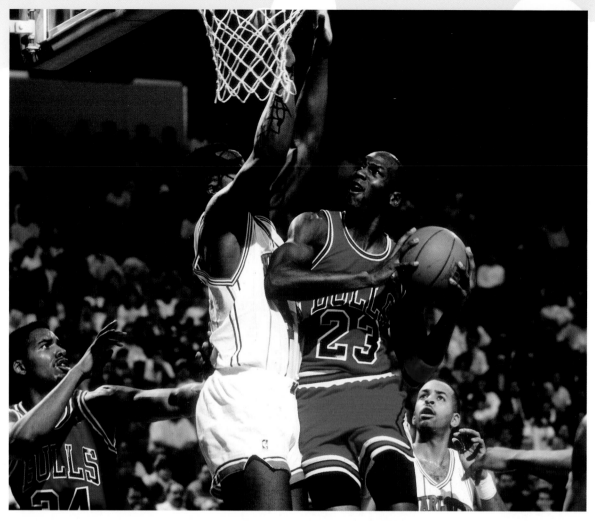

Michael Jordan, considered one of the greatest basketball players of all time, started his career with the Chicago Bulls in 1984.

The National Hockey League's Blackhawks have been Chicago's ice hockey team since 1926.

The Chicago Bears play football at Soldier Stadium. It is in Grant Park. They have won eight National Football League (NFL) championships and one Super Bowl.

The Chicago Bulls play basketball. This team has had some of the best basketball players in the world. They've won six National Basketball Association (NBA) championships.

Things to Do

The Brookfield Zoo is one of the largest zoos in the United States. More than 5,900 animals call it home. It was one of the first zoos to use ditches instead of cages to keep animals and people apart.

At Chicago's Museum of Science and **Industry**, you can crawl into a submarine, learn about robots, and even play tic-tac-toe with one.

The Museum of Science and Industry is the last building left from the World's Columbian Exposition of 1893. It holds over 2,000 exhibits.

Many famous writers and actors started at small Chicago theaters, like the Steppenwolf.

Comedy is big business in Chicago. Many famous people started at Second City, a comedy theater. After acting here, some starred in movies or television shows, such as Steve Carell and Bill Murray. Others have also become comedy writers, like Tina Fey and Stephen Colbert.

Taste of Chicago in Grant Park is the world's biggest food festival.

Many of Chicago's festivals include music. Chicago's Labor Day weekend jazz festival is world famous. Lollapalooza features rock concerts at Grant Park, and so much is going on, you might have to listen to two concerts at once.

Something interesting is always happening in the Windy City!

Timeline

1673
French explorers Marquette and Joliet reach Chicago area.

1803
Fort Dearborn built.

1848
Illinois and Michigan Canal opens a water route to New Orleans. Chicago gets its first railroad. McCormick opens first factory to build reapers, big farm machines.

1868
Marshall Field's department store opened.

1872
Montgomery Ward begins mail-order catalog.

1892
First "L" or elevated railway opens.

1900
Chicago River's direction is reversed.

1908
The last time Chicago Cubs win baseball's World Series.

1916
Navy Pier built.

1973
Sears Tower completed.

1779
Jean Baptiste Point du Sable settles in the Chicago area.

1837
Chicago officially becomes a city.

1861
Civil War begins and Chicago industry grows quickly.

1871
Great Chicago Fire burns for 2 days causing massive destruction and death.

1885
First skyscraper, The Home Insurance Building, built in Chicago.

1893
World's Columbian Exposition of 1893.

1906
White Sox beat the Chicago Cubs in baseball's World Series.

1926
Midway Airport opens.

1955
Chicago-O'Hare International Airport opens to public.

2008
Soon-to-be President Barack Obama gives victory speech in Grant Park.

Glossary

catalogs (KAT-uh-lawgs): magazines that show pictures of the goods you can buy from a company

factories (FAK-tur-ees): places where large amounts of something are made by workers and machines

immigrants (IM-i-gruhnts): people who moved from one country to settle in another one

industry (IN-duh-stree): factories (manufacturing) and other businesses

jazz (jaz): a type of American music that African-Americans began playing around 1900

neighborhoods (NAY-bur-huds): sections of a city where people live

pier (peer): a wooden or concrete platform built over water often where boats load and unload

skyscrapers (skye-skray-purz): very tall buildings that use a steel skeleton

swamp (swahmp): ground that stays wet and never drains completely

Index

Show What You Know

1. Chicago is near which bodies of water?
2. How did Chicago change after the Great Chicago Fire?
3. What is there to do in Chicago parks?
4. Why is Chicago sometimes called a "skyscraper museum?"
5. Where can you find Sue?

Websites to Visit

www.chicagohistory.org/mychicago/08kids.html

www.czs.org/Brookfield-ZOO/Zoo-Animals

www.sheddaquarium.org/Animals--Care/Animal-Facts

About the Author

Hilarie Staton spent a few years living in the Chicago area. She loved its museums, theaters, festivals, stores, and people. She did not love its cold, windy, snowy winter weather. She did have a lot of fun leading tours at the Chicago History Museum. She learned all about Chicago's history and especially old time radio. She has written many books for kids.

Meet The Author!
www.meetREMauthors.com

www.rourkeeducationalmedia.com

PHOTO CREDITS: Cover: © Pgiam, Songquan Deng, Dejan Jovanovic; Page 1: © Ferran Traité Soler; Page 3: © Gio_banfi; Page 4: © Mark Slusarczyk; Page 5: © Alan scottwalker; Page 6: © rabbit75can; Page 7: © Todd Patterson; Page 8: © Christopher Arndt; Page 9 & 10: © Thomas Barrat; Page 11: © Yin Yang, John Zocco; Page 12: © R.Gino Santa Maria; Page 13: © patty_c, rafalkrakow; Page 14: © compucon; Page 15: © Library of Congress; Page 16: © The Project Guttenburg/Wikipedia; Page 17 & 18: © Steve Geer; Page 19: © Wikipedia, Stefiross; Page 20: © Wikipedia; Page 21: © Davel5957; Page 22: © Scott Olson; Page 23: © Paweligaul; Page 24: © kubrak78; Page 25: © Jerry Coli; Page 26: Henryk Sadura; Page 27: © Victorgrigas; Page 28: © James Anderson; Page 29: © Jenwen, Steve Geer, Christopher Arndt, Alex Wong

© Edited by: Keli Sipperley

Illustrations by: Caroline Romanet

Cover and interior design by: Jen Thomas

Library of Congress PCN Data

Dropping in on Chicago / Hilarie Staton
  ISBN 978-1-68191-406-0 (hard cover)
  ISBN 978-1-68191-448-0 (soft cover)
  ISBN 978-1-68191-486-2 (e-Book)
Library of Congress Control Number: 2015951572

Printed in the United States of America, North Mankato, Minnesota

Also Available as:

ROURKE'S e-Books